How to use this book

Follow the advice, in italics, given for teachers on each page.
Praise *the children at every step!*

Detailed guidance is provided in the Read Write Inc. Phonics Handbook

8 reading activities

Children:
- *Practise reading the speed sounds.*
- *Read the green and red words for the story.*
- *Listen as you read the introduction.*
- *Discuss the vocabulary check with you.*
- *Read the story.*
- *Re-read the story and discuss the 'questions to talk about'.*
- *Re-read the story with fluency and expression.*
- *Practise reading the speed words.*

Speed sounds

Consonants *Say the pure sounds (do not add 'uh').*

f (ff)	l (ll)	m	n	r	s	v	z / s	sh	(th)	(ng) / nk

b	c / k / ck	d	g	h	j	p	qu	t	w (wh)	x	y	ch (tch)

Vowels *Say the sounds in and out of order.*

at	hen	in	on	up	day	see	high	blow	zoo

*Each box contains one sound but sometimes more than one grapheme. Focus graphemes are **circled**.*

Green words

wi<u>tch</u>   o<u>ff</u>   wi<u>ll</u>   <u>wh</u>isk   <u>th</u>en

wi<u>ng</u>   mo<u>th</u>   slug

cob`web → cobweb

Red words

<u>the</u>   <u>you</u>   I   s<u>ai</u>d   be   of   my

Vocabulary check

Discuss the meaning (as used in the story) after the children have read each word.

	definition:
cast	*make a spell (I will cast a spell on you.)*
wand	*magic stick used to cast spells (I will whisk my wand)*
moth	*night time butterfly (The wing of a moth)*
slug	*a snail without a shell (a fat slug)*
whisk	*wave (I will whisk my wand)*
cobweb	*a spider's trap*

Punctuation to note in this story:

Stitch	*Capital letter for the name of the witch.*
A You The Six Mix	*Capital letters that start sentences*
.	*Full stop at the end of each sentence.*
!	*Exclamation mark used to show anger and surprise*
...	*Wait and see*

The spell

Introduction

Who is the tidiest person in your house?
Meet Stitch the witch. She is a very fussy witch and likes
her home to be clean and tidy. Stitch the witch is cross
because her cat has left paw marks on her bed.

So rather than just tell her off (like your mum and dad
would do if you had made your bed spread dirty) she casts
a spell on the poor cat!

Story written by Gill Munton
Illustrated by Tim Archbold

"You bad cat!"
said Stitch the witch.

"I will cast a spell on you!
I will whisk my wand.
Then you will be ...
a frog!"

The wing of a moth ...
in the pot!

Six cobwebs ...
in the pot!

The leg **of** a rat ...
in **the** pot!

A fat slug ...
in **the** pot!

"Mix it up, mix it up ...

abracadabra!"

Ping!

Questions to talk about

FIND IT QUESTIONS

✓ *Turn to the page*

✓ *Read the question*

✓ *Find the answer*

Page 9: *What did Stitch the witch want her spell to do?*

What does the cat think to this?
(horrified / surprised / frightened)

Page 10-11: *What did Stitch put into the pot?*

Page 13: *What happened in the end?*

What do you think the cat is feeling now?
(pleased / relieved / 'that'll serve you right')